THE

DomEsDay

PROJECT BOOK

Elizabeth Hallam

Assistant Keeper of Public Records

HODDER AND STOUGHTON

LONDON   SYDNEY   AUCKLAND   TORONTO

Before 1066

Domesday Book was written 900 years ago, in 1086, but the reasons why it was written lie further back. A good place to begin the story is 1066, which is famous for being the year in which William the Conqueror won the Battle of Hastings and became King of England. But many other important events happened in the months before. It all began in January when Edward the Confessor, who had ruled for twenty-four years, died leaving no direct heir to succeed him. He left a land that would seem very primitive and dangerous to us today.

The England Edward ruled

Life for most people in Edward's England was very hard. Adults rarely lived longer than 30 years and many children didn't survive infancy. People suffered from unpleasant diseases for which there were no known cures and hygiene was very primitive. Food was coarse, unvaried and often scarce. The peasants lived in houses made of wood, wattle and daub – in many areas only churches were built of stone.

Laws were strict and harsh, and crimes were punishable by heavy fines, mutilation or death. Instead of proving an accused person's guilt with evidence (as today), for some crimes courts demanded that the person prove his or her innocence by undergoing an **ordeal**. Either he would have to clasp a red-hot iron bar in his hand and walk a certain number of steps, or he would plunge his hand into boiling water to take out a stone. If the injuries had begun to heal in three days, the person was innocent; if not, he was guilty and might be put to death - perhaps by hanging.

A medieval hanging.

However, compared with other European countries at the time, England was wealthy and well-governed. By 1000 it had become one kingdom and much of it had already been divided into counties. The boundaries of these survived with few changes right up to 1974. In charge of each was a **sheriff** who looked after the royal lands, administered justice and supervised the collection of tax. The tax, **danegeld**, was very valuable to the king. In 1018 the then enormous sum of £92,000 was collected, all in silver pennies.

These are silver pennies from the reign of Edward the Confessor.

England and Scandinavia

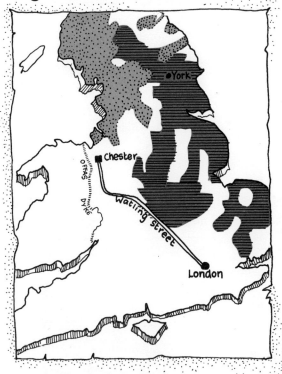

England's fertile lands and her wealth acted as a magnet to her neighbours, and since the 860s people from Scandinavia had raided, fought and then settled here. The Norwegians came mainly to the north-west, the Danes to the north-east and East Anglia. The settlers had their own languages, customs and laws, and the place names in these **Danelaw** areas are still Scandinavian in origin. From 1016 to 1042, England was ruled by Canute, King of Denmark, and his sons, as part of a Scandinavian empire, but in 1042 the West Saxon dynasty returned with Edward the Confessor. He was called back from exile in Normandy to become King of England.

Areas of strong Danish settlement

Areas of strong Norwegian settlement

Things to find out and do

1 Life in England during Edward's reign sounds very hard to us today. Can you think of any *good* things about life then that are not so good today? Think about things you don't like today and try to find out if they were better then. What about the natural world, for example? See if you can find ten good points about life in 1066.

2 Find out about the origins of the place names in your area. There are books that will help you. Does it seem that there were a lot of Scandinavian settlements? You could draw a map to show the different place name origins in the area.

3 What is there in and around the town or village where you live that was there in 1066? Hills and rivers may be unchanged but are you sure? That hill may be a grassed-over slag heap; a stream may have been diverted to make way for a factory. See if you can find out. Some things that seem less solid can be older. This oak tree, for example, is thought to be 1,000 years old. It was 100 years old even in 1066!

Edwinstowe Major oak

1066 – the claimants and the battles

When Edward the Confessor died on 5 January 1066 leaving no heir to succeed him, there were several people with a good claim to the throne of England.

Harold Hardraada, King of Norway. His father had been promised rights to England by one of King Canute's sons.

Swein Estrithson, King of Denmark. He was King Canute's nephew and a rival of Harold Hardraada. (He was to invade England in 1069 and was beaten only with great difficulty.)

William, Duke of Normandy.
He was descended from the Viking warlords who had conquered and settled Normandy in the early tenth century, and he was related, although not closely, to the West Saxon royal house. Edward the Confessor knew and trusted William and for much of his reign favoured him as his successor.

Harold swears an oath to support Duke William as Edward's successor.

Edgar Aetheling, a West Saxon prince who never found enough support for his claim.

Earl Harold Godwineson, the leading English earl. He and his family stood out against William's succession, but in 1062 he was sent to Normandy, probably to confirm the Confessor's pledge to his rival. He had, William later claimed, sworn a solemn and binding oath to accept the Norman duke as king.

On his deathbed, Edward the Confessor changed his mind and named Earl Harold as his successor. Harold, with the support of many of the English nobility, was crowned as King of England on the day of Edward's funeral.

The battles

King Harold's enemies and rivals soon began to gather their armies together. In September, Harold Hardraada landed in the north of England and defeated Earls Edwin and Morcar at the battle of Fulford Gate. King Harold rushed north and in a spectacular victory crushed the unprepared Norwegian forces at Stamford Bridge. That was on September 25th. Three days later, Duke William landed at Pevensey with a large army of northern French troops, not knowing which King Harold he would have to fight for the English throne.

As soon as he had heard about William's arrival, King Harold hurried south again. Leaving his exhausted army little time to recover, he tried to surprise William. But the duke was ready, and on 14th October 1066 he attacked Harold and his men near Hastings before they were fully in battle order.

Harold's army, numbering about 7,000, had the strong position of Battle hill to defend. All depended on the **housecarls,** the highly trained warriors who formed a shield wall and fought with javelins and axes. William's slightly smaller forces relied on archers and on knights on horseback. The Anglo-Saxons proved hard to break, and, perhaps as a ruse, some of the Normans fled in confusion. Many of the English, thinking the victory was theirs, rushed after them, only to be cut to pieces by the Norman knights.

William's forces then attacked the main Anglo-Saxon army and defeated it, leaving several thousands dead. Among them was King Harold, who was shot in the eye by an arrow. William, the Conqueror, was crowned in his place on Christmas Day 1066.

William later founded a monastery on the site of the battle of Hastings, partly to atone for all the killing. But its unusual name, Battle Abbey, and its siting on the battlefield (high, waterless, and inconvenient for monks) suggest that the king wanted it also to be a reminder of his victory.

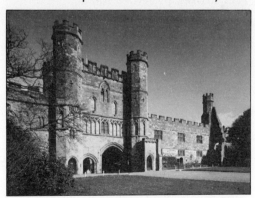

The gatehouse of Battle Abbey today.

Things to find out and do

Several of the pictures above are taken from the famous Bayeux Tapestry. What is happening in the border of the tapestry showing Harold's death? You could design a long picture, or frieze, to show either a series of important national events or something much simpler – a day in your life, perhaps. Don't forget to show details of various kinds in the borders of your design.

Changes the Normans made

Soon after the Conquest, William began to make changes to the way that England was governed. There were four main changes.

1 He took away most of the land from the Anglo-Saxon **thegns** and divided it between his Norman and other followers. The Anglo-Saxon earldoms, which had been almost like small kingdoms, were split up, and the great Norman estates were scattered throughout England.

2 After the Conquest, all land in theory belonged to the king. The great nobles were his tenants, and they let out land to lesser nobles and knights. Look at the feudal ladder on the next page to see how this worked.

   In return for his land, each tenant swore that he would be loyal and obedient to his lord (he did **homage** and swore **fealty**). The tenant also had to send knights to serve in the lord's army. Before 1066 such feudal arrangements had been rare and much land had been **allodial** (owned like modern freehold land).

3 Normans replaced English people in the top posts – as earls, sheriffs and bishops. The change was far more sudden for the earls and sheriffs, because Edward the Confessor had already brought in some French bishops before 1066.

A knight does homage to his lord.

4 Norman French was spoken at the king's court and Latin replaced English as the language of government. Domesday Book was to be written in Latin.

Things to find out and do

1 Think carefully about the feudal ladder on the next page. Does anyone that you see on it still own land today? See if you can find out where the Queen owns land, for example.
2 Norman French has entered our language in many areas of life. On page 26 you will see how some French words came to be used for items of food, for example. Try to find out other groups of words that came from French. You will need a large dictionary that gives the origins of words as well as their meanings. Can you tell from your collection which areas of life the Normans influenced most?

The feudal ladder

After 1066, the system of government divided people into groups as shown on the feudal ladder below. All these groups are mentioned in Domesday Book but some of the terms, whether Norman or English in origin, seem strange to us today.

Freemen were men who were free but who owed some services to their lords.

Sokemen were like freemen, but they also had to attend their lords' courts. Freemen and sokemen made up 12% of the recorded population and were concentrated in the Danelaw counties.

Villeins were the highest class of unfree peasants, who owed their lords labour services but who also farmed lands for themselves.

Bordars and **cottars** were cottagers — unfree peasants who had less land than the villeins. Villeins, bordars and cottars were found all over England and made up 72% of the recorded population.

Slaves were the property of their lords and had no lands. Of the recorded population, 10% were enslaved. They were mainly in the southern and western counties.

Burgesses were people who lived in boroughs as described on pages 22 and 23.

The other 2% of the recorded population was made up of many different categories, including priests, swineherds, Frenchmen, knights and steersmen.

The Domesday population

Domesday Book gives us an incomplete picture of the population of England in 1086. Most women, children, nobles, retainers, monks and nuns are omitted. The actual number of people mentioned in Domesday is 268,300, but England's total population in 1086 was between 1½ and 2 million, about half the level it had reached in Roman times.

How Domesday Book was made

In the middle ages, books were rare and precious objects that could be read only by the few educated people, who were mostly **clerks** (people in holy orders). Books were written either on **parchment** (sheep skin) as Domesday Book was, or on **vellum** (cattle skin). The skins had to be prepared very carefully. They were washed, dipped in lime, washed again, and stretched out on a wooden frame to dry. The surface was then scraped and rubbed with pumice to make it smooth, and the skins were next trimmed into shape. Booklets known as **quires** were made up from about four folded sheets, and each page was ruled so that the **scribes** could write neatly and evenly. After all the writing and **illumination** (decoration) had been completed, the booklets were carefully bound up in order.

Pens and ink

The Domesday scribes wrote with quill pens made from the large wing feathers of birds. They used **ferrogallotannate ink**, made from galls (produced by oak trees), gum arabic and ferrous sulphate, and perhaps mixed with wine or beer. This was colourless when made but turned black when exposed to the air. Over the centuries it has faded to brown.

A medieval scribe at work.

The Domesday handwriting

Both volumes of Domesday Book are written in the style of handwriting known as **Caroline minuscule**. It had been developed by an Englishman, Alcuin, at the court of the Emperor Charlemagne in about AD 800, and was widely used for several centuries. It is a clear, neat script that is easy to read, and is the direct ancestor of printed lettering today. Domesday's capital letters are called **rustic capitals**. They are used for headings and are usually written or underlined in red. This process, known as **rubrication**, is meant to guide the reader's eye to the important information, such as the names of the counties.

Through the centuries, many extracts from Domesday Book have been used as evidence in court cases. Between about 1470 and 1715, Domesday's keepers wrote these copies in a mock-Domesday script. This was a sign of their admiration for King William's great survey.

Rex ten̄ bruderione 7 bere Colesberie 7 Sapecone 7 Bere potte 7 Cidihoc...

Why 'Domesday Book'?

'Domesday' was a hostile nickname given to the book by the native Anglo-Saxons, probably soon after the work was completed. They called it 'Domesday Book' because it reminded them of the terrifying idea of the Last Judgement in the Bible, as described in Revelation and painted on the walls of many churches. By the 1170s the king's servants, who liked the name, had also begun to use it to replace titles like 'the king's book' or 'the Winchester roll', and since the 1220s it has been known as 'Domesday Book' in all government documents.

Things to find out and do

1 Make some ink using a pre-Domesday recipe. Mix carbon (as in soot) with a little water and a little glue. Experiment until you get it to the right thickness, then try it out with an old-fashioned dip pen, or with a quill if you can find a suitable feather.

2 Make some mock parchment by crumpling a piece of plain paper up into a ball and dipping it for a few minutes into a bowl of cold tea. Then unfold the paper and leave it to dry. When it is dry, smooth the paper out and it will look like ancient parchment. If you can find an adult to help you and are very careful, you can burn just the edges of the paper with a lighted match to give a really old effect.

3 Look at the passage of Domesday writing above. Try to copy the letter shapes, letter by letter. Then write words and whole sentences. Finally use your own dip or quill pen, your medieval ink and your 'parchment' to write a page to display on your wall.

4 Look up the passage in the Bible describing the Last Judgement and you will see why, to people who were not familiar with books and could not read, the book described in the Bible might seem to be like King William's frightening survey. You will find the passage in Revelation (the last book of the Bible), chapter 20, verses 11-13.

The survey – why and how?

William was a harsh and firm ruler of England and he had many enemies. Defending his lands was expensive and by Christmas 1085 he had probably decided to hold a survey to find out exactly what lands and resources all his subjects had in England. Then he could tax them to the full and make sure that no one escaped from paying him. A survey would also help to settle disputes about who should own certain lands, and would help to satisfy the Conqueror's curiosity about his kingdom. William therefore ordered that a full investigation be made as quickly as possible. Domesday Book was to be the record that summarised all this material.

Domesday Counties and Circuits

Finding out about England

All the tenants-in-chief (the great men of the country) and the sheriffs were first asked to send in details about their lands. They were to say what each manor was worth and who their tenants were. The next task was to divide England into groups of counties, now called **circuits.**

The king then chose three or four **commissioners** to supervise more detailed inquiries in each circuit. These were rich and powerful men, mainly Normans, who went from county to county with an armed escort and made the people of each village come to the courts and answer questions about their lands. The huge amount of information this produced was carefully cross-checked and summarised into the **circuit returns**.

The questions

What is the manor called?
Who held it in the time of King Edward and who holds it now?
How many ploughs does the lord have and how many do the men have?
How many villeins, bordars, cottars and slaves are there?
How many freemen and sokemen are there?
How much woodland, meadow and pasture is there?
How many mills and fisheries are there?
What has been added to or taken away from the estate?
What was it worth in 1066 and what is it worth now?
What lands do the freemen and sokemen have?
Can any more money or produce be taken from the estate?

Writing Domesday Book

King William was probably given the finished circuit returns on 1 August 1086, when he was at Salisbury. Among these returns were the manuscripts now known as **Little Domesday**, covering Essex, Norfolk and Suffolk, and the **Exeter Domesday**, which describes Cornwall, Devon and other south-western counties. The second stage of summarising now began. A trusted scribe, probably an Englishman, but whose name we don't know, was set to work to compile **Great Domesday**, a more convenient shortened version of all the circuit returns, leaving out many details. He was given his orders by a Norman scribe whose handwriting may be seen in Great Domesday in a few places. This Norman might have been King William's chaplain, Samson, who was later to become the Bishop of Worcester.

When King William died, in September 1087, the two scribes had already worked through all the circuit returns except for Little Domesday. The making of Great Domesday stopped, and it was decided to keep Little Domesday as part of the final record. Both volumes were bound up as books within a few years of William's death.

Things to find out and do

1 Are the questions that the commissioners asked the ones that you would have asked? Do you think that there are other things that King William should have tried to find out? Make a list of them.

2 Make a list of all the questions *you* would like to ask people in 1086 if you could travel back in time. Your questions will probably be about what life was like in Norman times, but William, of course, knew about that!

3 What will people in the future want to know about us? See if you can list the questions that will be asked about our lives in 900 years' time.

4 When you have thought about what people in the future will want to know about us, decide upon ten items that you could seal in a box to be opened in 900 years' time.

Two Domesday manors: Bakewell

Great Domesday, folios 272v, 273, 274.

The Domesday Book entry

and Hartington, Derbyshire

Translation

(LAND OF THE KING. High Peak wapentake.)
In BAKEWELL with its eight **berewicks**[1] King Edward had 18
carucates[2] of **geldable**[3] land. Land for **18 ploughs.**[4] Now the King has on the
demesne[5]
7 ploughs, and 33 villeins and 9 bordars. There are 2 priests and a church **and under
them there are**[6] 2 villeins and 5 bordars who together have 11 ploughs. 1 knight has 16
acres of land
and 2 bordars. There is one mill **(worth)**[7] **10s.8d**[8] and 1 lead mine
and 80 acres of meadow. **Underwood**[9] **1 league long**[10] and 1 wide. Of this land
3 carucates belong to the Church. Henry Ferrars claims 1 carucate in Haddon.
These are the BEREWICKS of this manor: (Nether) Haddon, Holme, Rowsley, Burton,
Conkesbury, One Ash, Monyash, (Over) Haddon....

These three manors (Bakewell, Ashford and Hope) in the time of King Edward
rendered[11] £30 and
5½ **sesters**[12] of honey and 5 cartloads of 50 lead slabs.
Now they render £10.6s. William Peverel has charge of them.

(LAND OF HENRY FERRARS. Wirksworth wapentake.)
In HARTINGTON Godwin and Ligulf had 2 carucates of geldable land.
There is land for 2 ploughs. It is **waste.**[13] There are 16 acres of meadow, underwood
3 **furlongs**[14] long and 2 wide. In the time of King Edward **it was worth**[15] 40s.

Key

1 Outlying part of a manor. 2 Taxable unit of land, of a size which could be ploughed by 1
ploughteam (so the acreage varied). Often 120 acres (49 hectares). In areas outside the
Danelaw, the equivalent term was 'hide'. 3 Land paying the geld tax. 4 This figure is
probably a tax assessment. 5 On the lord's part of the manor. 6 = 'who hold'. 7 The
amount which the lord could expect to receive each year. 8 10 shillings and 8 pence
(about 57p). 9 Coppiced wood. 10 About 3 modern miles. 11 Paid to the king. 12 About
32 ounces (905 grams). 13 Uncultivated (this place had been devastated by King William
in 1069). 14 220 yards (just over 200 metres), the length of the average ploughed furrow.
15 But it was worth nothing in 1086.

Domesday Book facts – true or false?

Ever since the later middle ages people have thought that Domesday Book could tell them what they wanted to know about any matter concerned with lands, rights or pedigrees. In the fourteenth century, some peasants thought that if they bought copies of parts of the book, they would have to work less hard. In 1661 Samuel Pepys tried to find out about the sea from it. People still try to look up their family trees there and are disappointed not to find them.

Some of the statements about Domesday Book below are true and some are false. Can *you* tell which are which? When you have checked your answers on page 32, test your family and friends as well.

Domesday Book is:

1 a complete description of life in the late eleventh century.

2 a population census.

3 a book of family trees.

4 an illuminated manuscript.

5 arranged county by county.

6 a book containing about 2 million words.

7 a description of 13,418 places in 37 pre-1974 counties.

8 in two volumes, Great Domesday and Little Domesday, now bound up in five parts.

True...
insert number from above :

False...
insert number from above :

Things to find out and do

1 The family tree on the next pages shows how William the Conqueror was distantly related to King Harold. Look carefully at the family tree and draw a ring around all the people that are mentioned in this book. Then draw a different coloured ring around all the Kings of England on the tree. You will see that the question of the succession to the throne was a very complicated one.

2 You have already looked at place names and their origins. What about first names of people? Look carefully at the family tree again and make two lists. In one of them put all the names that sound strange to you today; in the other list put all the names that you could imagine a person being called today. Are you surprised by the result? See if you can find out where the names still in use today came from originally. Were they already old in 1066? Can you think of any reason why some names last and others do not?

3 Do a survey of the names of your friends or the people in your class. Collect as many names as possible. Then ask all your friends to find out their parents' first names. The list will probably be different from that of your friends' names. When you have completed all your work on names, can you compile a historical top ten for boys' and girls' names?

4 Have you ever drawn a family tree? You will need to ask your parents and relatives for information about members of your family in the past and if you find this interesting you might like to take your research further and look at gravestones and records of people even further back. There are books about how to go about this that would help you. In the meantime, why not concentrate on making your family tree as *wide* as possible? Try to put on all your cousins and even more distant relatives. It is more interesting if you also write something about each of the people, like this:

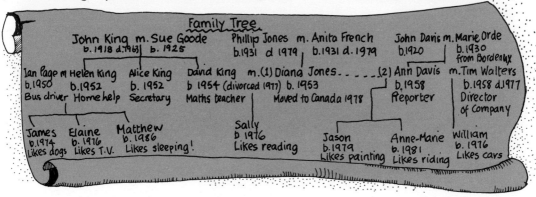

Family Tree

John King m. Sue Goode   Phillip Jones m. Anita French   John Davis m. Marie Orde
b.1918 d.1963   b. 1925   b.1931 d 1979 , b.1931 d. 1979   b.1920   b.1930 from Bordeaux

Ian Page m Helen King   Alice King   David King m.(1) Diana Jones. . . . . (2) Ann Davis m.Tim Walters
b.1950   b.1952   b. 1952   b 1954 (divorced 1977) b.1953   b.1958   b.1958 d.1977
Bus driver   Home help   Secretary   Maths teacher | Moved to Canada 1978   Reporter   Director of Company

James   Elaine   Matthew   Sally   Jason   Anne-Marie   William
b.1974   b.1976   b.1986   b 1976   b.1979   b.1981   b. 1976
Likes dogs   Likes T.V.   Likes sleeping!   Likes reading   Likes painting   Likes riding   Likes cars

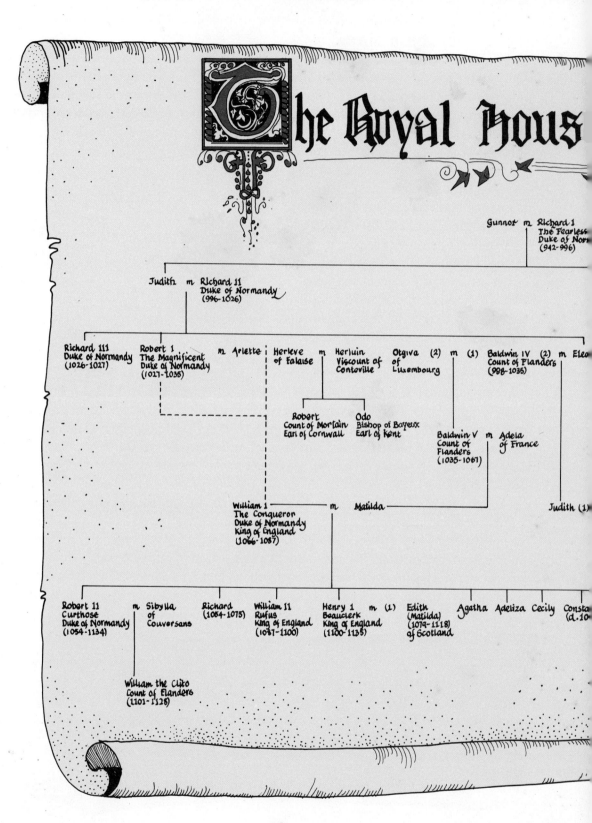

Gunnor m Richard 1
The Fearless
Duke of Nor
(942-996)

Judith m Richard 11
Duke of Normandy
(996-1026)

Richard 111
Duke of Normandy
(1026-1027)

Robert 1
The Magnificent
Duke of Normandy
(1027-1035)

m Arlette

Herleve
of Falaise

m Herluin
Viscount of
Contoville

Otgiva (2) m (1) Baldwin IV (2) m Eleo
of
Luxembourg

Count of Flanders
(988-1035)

Robert
Count of Mortain
Earl of Cornwall

Odo
Bishop of Bayeux
Earl of Kent

Baldwin V m Adela
Count of
Flanders
(1035-1067)

of France

William 1
The Conqueror
Duke of Normandy
King of England
(1066-1087)

m Matilda

Judith (1

Robert 11
Curthose
Duke of Normandy
(1054-1134)

m Sibylla
of
Couversans

Richard
(1054-1075)

William 11
Rufus
King of England
(1087-1100)

Henry 1 m (1)
Beauclerk
King of England
(1100-1135)

Edith
(Matilda)
(1079-1118)
of Scotland

Agatha Adeliza Cecily Consta
(d.10

William the Clito
Count of Flanders
(1101-1128)

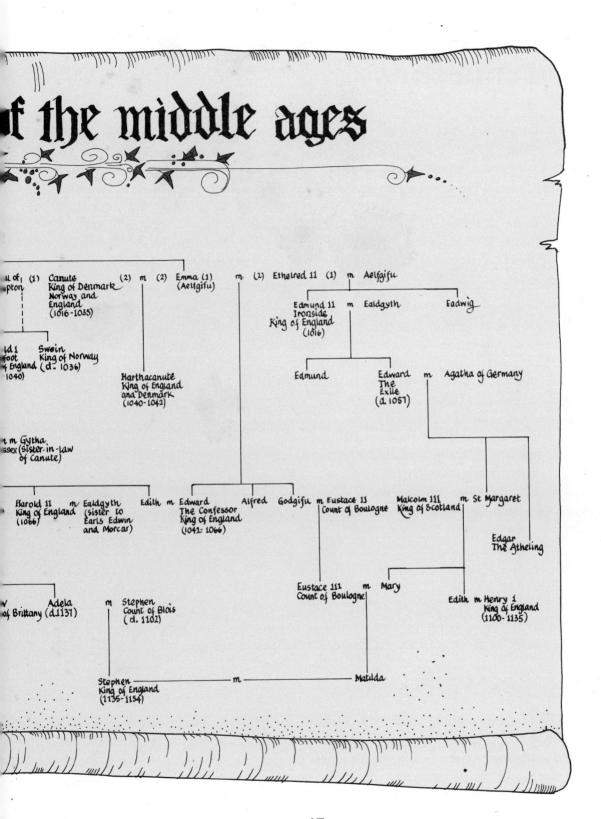

...u of | (1) Canute   (2) m (2) Emma (1)   m (2) Ethelred 11 (1) m Aelfgifu
...pton   King of Denmark   (Aelfgifu)
               Norway and   Edmund 11 m Ealdgyth   Eadwig
               England   Ironside
               (1016-1035)   King of England
                                                             (1016)

...d 1   Swein
...foot   King of Norway
...England (d. 1036)   Edmund   Edward   m Agatha of Germany
(1040)   The
               Harthacanute   Exile
               King of England   (d. 1051)
               and Denmark
               (1040-1042)

...n m Gytha
...ssex (sister-in-law
       of Canute)

 Harold 11   m Ealdgyth   Edith m Edward   Alfred   Godgifu m Eustace 11   Malcolm 111   m St Margaret
 King of England (sister to   The Confessor   Count of Boulogne King of Scotland
 (1066)   Earls Edwin   King of England
                and Morcar)   (1041-1066)
                                                                                                    Edgar
                                                                                                    The Atheling

                                                     Eustace 111   m Mary
                                                     Count of Boulogne
...y   Adela   m Stephen   Edith m Henry 1
...of Brittany (d.1137)   Count of Blois   King of England
                          (d. 1102)   (1100-1135)

               Stephen ————————————————— m —————————————— Matilda
               King of England
               (1135-1154)

The Norman landscape – castles and churches

Some of the changes that the Normans made can still be seen today. To show the conquered English who was in charge, they built castles all over the country. Before 1066 these had been a rarity. The new castles were intended to protect their lords from hostile neighbours and to frighten and dominate the local peasants. Archaeologists have found almost 2,500 castles that were built during the whole Norman period (1066–1154). Many of them were small and temporary, and all but a few are now completely or partly ruined.

Norman castles had a **motte**, or flat-topped mound, at the centre, with a strong wooden stockade and a great wooden tower at the top. There was a **ditch** around the motte with a **drawbridge** across it. Beyond that was the **bailey**, a lower enclosure surrounding the motte. It too had a ditch and **palisade** around it, and it contained the living accommodation for the people, storehouses and stables for the horses. If during a siege this part of the castle was captured, the defenders could retreat to the motte for their last stand.

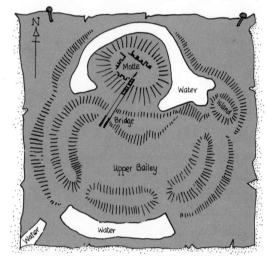

A plan of Pleshey Castle, one of the ruined Norman castles that can be visited today.

A few Norman castles had rectangular stone keeps (towers) and stone walls to make them exceptionally strong. King William's most famous stone castle is the White Tower in the Tower of London, begun soon after the Conquest to impress and terrify the people of one of England's most important cities. The king had the white stone with which it is built brought across the Channel specially from Caen in Normandy.

Things to find out and do

1 Draw a picture or make a model of a Norman castle as you think it might have looked soon after it was built. How easy would it have been to besiege a castle? Why were stone towers preferable to wooden ones?
2 If there is a Norman castle near you, try to go and visit it. Imagine what it would have been like to live there. You could write a play about life in a besieged castle.

Churches

The Normans also brought a new style of church building with them. The walls were massive, sometimes as much as six metres thick at the bottom, and far bigger than those made by the Anglo-Saxons. There were large round pillars and round arches; towers were square and squat; and ceilings were either flat and wooden or covered in a stone **barrel vault**

In the next century, Norman churches became more lavishly decorated. A typical feature is the **chevron (dogtooth) pattern** as shown here. By 1200 another major change was already underway as the Norman style gave way to **Gothic**. With its pointed arches, larger windows and thinner walls, this very different from the dark and massive buildings of the Conqueror's day.

Domesday book mentions 2,287 places with priests or parish churches, although we know from other documents that this number is only about one fifth of the total that existed at the time. In 1086 many churches were owned by **lay lords**, who took rents from them – this is why they are listed in the book among the possessions of manors. Sometimes Domesday provides details about the buildings. At Netheravon in Wiltshire, the old church was ruined, roofless and about to fall down, but at Bermondsey in Surrey, there was a new and beautiful church.

Things to find out and do

1 Visit churches near your home and see if you can spot whether they have Norman parts or not. Use the drawings on this page to give you clues. Remember that the Victorians copied medieval styles in their churches. Can you tell the genuine Norman features from more modern ones? When you have visited a church, check afterwards to see if you were right about the Norman parts. Many churches have a leaflet for visitors to tell them about the special features and history of the church, so you will be able to check on the spot. Don't check until you have looked around yourself though!

2 Visit some really modern churches. Do you prefer them to older styles? What do you think churches will look like in the future? You could try designing your own.

Life in the Domesday village

The lives of the Domesday villagers revolved around the agricultural calendar. Women and children as well as men had to help in the fields, especially at busy times of the year. There was also livestock to be tended, houses to be built and repaired, clothes to be made, water to be fetched and food to be prepared and cooked. With none of the gadgets and mass-produced goods of today, it took people most of their time simply to feed and clothe themselves.

One centre of village life was the **hall**, the building where the lord of the manor's court was held. Here too the lord's **bailiff** (the official who ran the manor's finances) and the **reeve** (the official in charge of agricultural work, who made sure that the peasants paid their dues) would organise the work of the manor.

Medieval peasants at work in the fields.

The **parish church** was the other centre of village life. It was a meeting-place as well as a place of worship. All the villagers went to the services (held in Latin) and observed the **feast days** and **fast days** in the Church's calendar (such as Christmas and Lent). Some parish priests were wealthy and respected figures; others were poor and joined in with the work in the fields. The church took a tenth of all produce in **tithes**, which were used to pay for parish priests, bishops and church buildings.

The fields

Many Domesday manors would have contained scattered settlements surrounded by a patchwork of small enclosed fields. But in some areas, particularly in the Midlands, the lords and peasants had already begun to replan their villages by moving their houses and gardens around a village green, and combining their **arable land** into two or three large open fields. These fields were divided into strips, which were shared between the lord and peasants according to their rank. The strips were usually ploughed towards their centres, making a ridged effect. One of the fields lay **fallow** and was used as **pasture**, while the rest was planted with grain and beans.

The ploughteam

The average size of a Domesday ploughteam was 8 oxen. In some entries half a plough is recorded, meaning that the team was shared with a manor nearby.

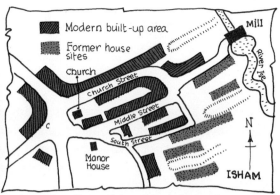

The ridged effect of strip farming can still be seen from the air today. These fields are in Warwickshire.

A plan of the village of Isham, Northamptonshire, unchanged in form since the time of Domesday.

The mill

Watermills were needed to grind wheat and barley into flour for bread, and Domesday mentions more than 6,000 of them. Windmills did not come to England for another 100 years.

How land was used in the 1080s

Arable land was ploughed and used to grow wheat, barley, oats and beans.
Pasture was land where animals – sheep, cattle, goats, horses – grazed all year round.
Meadows, often bordering streams, were cut for hay and used for grazing.
Waste was the name for land that was not fit for farming for some reason.
Woodland usually lay in small compact areas and was used for grazing pigs or for firewood. Large areas of woodland, such as the Weald or Cannock Chase, were rare.
Forest was the name for land reserved for the king's hunting, which could be wooded or open ground. People caught poaching could be mutilated (by, say, having their hands chopped off), or killed.

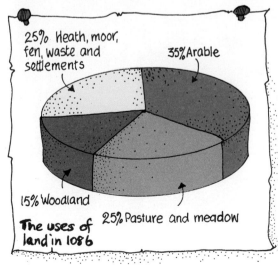

The uses of land in 1086

Things to find out and do

1 By using a map and walking around a small part of your local area, see if you can work out how the land is divided up now. If you live in a town, your pie chart may look very different from the one on the left. You may have to have sections for car parks, railways or sports grounds.
2 Why do you think oxen were used instead of horses for ploughing?
3 Try to visit a watermill. How does it work?

The Domesday boroughs

Domesday Book mentions people called **burgesses** in about 110 towns and manors. They were the people who had property and rights in their town and who attended a special court or courts with their own local laws and customs. It is settlements where burgesses lived that we now call **boroughs,** but there are other features that many eleventh-century boroughs shared.

Town walls

These had been built in some places as early as AD 900 and Domesday Book mentions them in several boroughs, including Stafford and Oxford. They made the borough a place of strength and defended its burgesses against attacks.

Markets

Many Domesday boroughs were important centres of trade, which could be both local and long-distance. Wine, wool and foodstuffs were among the items on sale in such markets. At Tutbury in Staffordshire 42 burgesses made their living totally from trade.

Mints

Coinage in the form of silver pennies was struck in the mints in many towns. The king allowed his moneyers to make the coins for him, and to take a profit from it in return for paying him a rent. At Lincoln this rent added up to £75 a year.

Life in the borough

The boroughs were traditionally under the control of the king or a tenant-in-chief, but by 1086 the burgesses in many towns were becoming increasingly independent. They lived on **messuages** (plots of land each containing a house and garden) but many also cultivated the fields outside the town. The life of the boroughs centred around the parish churches, markets, guilds and courts.

The king and local nobles usually owned some or many houses in the boroughs. At Warwick, King William had 113 houses out of a total of 225. The lord of a borough often had very considerable powers there. In Lincoln, the king had destroyed 116 houses to make way for his castle, and at Canterbury, 27 properties had been demolished to make way for a new palace for the archbishop.

The borough entries in Domesday vary a great deal in length and detail. The two most important towns in England, London and Winchester, are missing altogether, and others, like Bristol, get only a brief mention. Some borough descriptions seem to date from before 1066 and perhaps the decision to include the towns in the survey came only at a late stage, so that there was no time to find out newer information about them.

Here is an extract from the Domesday entry for the borough of Exeter in Devon.

IN THE CITY OF EXETER THE KING HAS 300 houses minus 15 rendering **customary dues**[1]. The city renders £18 a year. Of these Baldwin the Sheriff has £6 **weighed and tested for purity**[2] and Colwin £12 **in face value**[3] from the administration of Queen Edith's property.

In this city 48 houses have been laid waste since the king came to England.[4]

In the time of King Edward this city did not pay **geld**[5] except when London and York and Winchester paid geld, and that was **half a mark**[6] of silver for the use of the men-at-arms.

Key: 1 Making usual annual payments. 2 To make sure it was worth the full amount. 3 Not tested so could be damaged or impure. 4 1066. 5 Tax. 6 1 mark = 13s 4d (67p).

Things to find out and do

1 Find out whether your local towns had walls in the middle ages. Your local library or museum will tell you how to find out and may have maps showing what the town plan is thought to have been in those days.
2 Do you know which goods were traded in your area in the middle ages? There may be clues in street names or, again, your local library and museums may be able to help. Ask if there is a list of the present local businesses and shops, too, or do your own survey of industry and commerce in your area. Are there *any* similarities with the medieval pattern?
3 Try to design a coin yourself. The silver pennies of King William's time always had a cross on the back so that they could be clipped in halves and quarters. You could incorporate a similar feature in your design.

Silver pennies from the reign of King William.

Travel

Travel in Norman England was much more difficult and dangerous than it is today and many people never travelled more than a few miles from their homes in their whole lives. But there were some important reasons why difficult journeys were made.

To fight: armies on forced marches could cross England in a matter of days, as King Harold's did in 1066. In the 1090s many thousands of people travelled as far as Palestine in the armies of the First Crusade.

A medieval siege.

To trade: people might drive their animals to the local market, or they might bring in goods from other countries, such as wine from Germany or spices from the Far East.

On pilgrimage: many journeys were made to places as far afield as Rome, Santiago in Spain, or Jerusalem, so that pilgrims could visit shrines and other holy places.

The horse

People journeying overland for long distances depended greatly on horses. Although much slower than the cars and trains of today, they had the advantage that they could travel over the roughest ground and even swim through rivers where there were no bridges.

The Bayeux tapestry shows us how important mounted knights were in war. In 1066 the Normans' strong and stocky horses were shipped across the Channel with them. In the later middle ages, as armour grew heavier, so did the horses. The shire horses of today, such as the Suffolk Punch, are the direct descendants of the great medieval warhorses or **destriers**. Lighter horses, known as **palfreys** and **rounceys**, were used for riding and **sumpter horses**, as they were called, as pack animals.

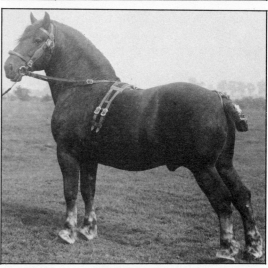

A Suffolk Punch stallion.

Roads

When the Romans were in Britain, they built many long, straight roads for their armies and traders, but many of these decayed in the Dark Ages, to be replaced by a complicated network of roads and tracks. By 1066 those had formed the general pattern which roads that are not motorways or bypasses still follow today. Roads were usually repaired at the expense of local people, although standards were very poor. The low-lying roads of 1086 were really just expanses of ruts, potholes and mud.

Rivers

When a road came to a river, a traveller usually had to **ford** the river by wading across it. Sometimes, however, there were bridges, although these were often owned by someone who charged a **toll** for travellers to cross them. In Chester, however, Domesday records that the people of the county paid for the upkeep of the bridge. Although rivers could be a barrier to the traveller, they could also be used as a quick and easy way to travel, as long as the water was deep enough for the shallow-bottomed boats. Domesday tells us that traffic on the River Trent at Nottingham was strictly controlled, with an £8 fine for blocking the way of boats.

The sea

We know what Norman ships looked like from the Bayeux tapestry. To us they seem small and flimsy, but they were the same basic design as those used by the Vikings when they made their long voyages to Iceland and Greenland. The ships had both sails and oars, but they were shallow and could carry very little cargo. The only way to get from England to Normandy was, of course, by sea. The crossing could be very dangerous, especially in winter, and many people were drowned. But the links between the kingdom and the duchy were so close that there was a great deal of cross-Channel traffic.

Things to find out and do

In 1086 there was only one way to cross the Channel. Find out how many different ways there are now. Do you think that there will be even more ways in 900 years' time? Imagine some future inventions and draw diagrams to show how they would work.

Domesday food and drink

Food for the rich

If you like rich, spicy food, you would probably have enjoyed the diet of the Domesday aristocracy. During the long winter months after the last of the spare animals had been killed to save fodder, meat could be kept fresh only by salting. As this had a nasty effect on its taste and texture, wine, nutmeg, cloves, pepper and other flavourings were added. By Lent (the five weeks leading up to Easter) meat had run very low, and anyway it was forbidden by the Church during this period. Fish, such as eel, herring, salmon and porpoise, was eaten instead, as on other fast days.

Although food was elegantly cooked and served, table manners were primitive by today's standards. People ate with their fingers, using only knives to cut their food, and bones were tossed to the dogs, which scavenged among the rushes on the floor. After the Conquest, English names for food were often replaced by French ones. Stew was called *pottage* (from *potage*), ox-meat was called *beef* (*boeuf*), sheep became *mutton* (*mouton*) and pig became *pork* (*porc*). A meat or fish mousse, *blancmanger*, was the ancestor of modern blancmange.

Food for the poor

Peasant food was rougher and plainer than that of the lords and ladies. Only the wealthier people would have eaten much meat (bacon or fowl) and during the winter even salted meat or fish could be hard to come by. Coarse bread, cheese, thick oatmeal, pea and bean soups and ale were the everyday diet of the villagers.

Domesday drinks

Ale was the most important drink in the England and Wales of 1086. Cider was not to be made for another century, but there were a few vineyards producing local wines. However, English wine was usually sharp and rough and the aristocracy preferred to ship in better-quality vintages from Germany and France.

Some Domesday livestock

Oxen and **Cattle** were important as draft animals and gave meat and hides.

Goats were the main providers of milk.

Pigs were an important source of meat.

Sheep grazed the hill areas in large numbers. They supplied England's famous wool, and would be eaten.

Poultry were needed for their eggs and for food.

Fish and **eels** were kept in special ponds or caught in the sea or river.

Bees produced honey, the only sweetener.

Things to find out and do

1 Try to recreate a Domesday garden in pots, windowboxes or your own garden at home. **Flowers:** grow lilies, roses, violets, peonies, daffodils and poppies. (Crush rose hips to make a delicious herbal tea and use the petals to make a *pot pourri*.)

Vegetables: grow cabbages, peas, leeks, onions, garlic, lettuce and pumpkins. Use your produce to make thick vegetable soups (pottages). (Vegetables had other uses too. Try boiling some onion skins in water with a piece of white cloth. What happens?)

Fruit: you can't grow apples and pears in a windowbox, but try to taste some older varieties of fruit, such as Cox's Orange Pippins, to get an idea of what even older varieties might have been like.

Herbs: grow parsley, fennel, coriander, sage, mint, feverfew, chervil and perhaps the bitter-tasting rue. Use them to flavour your cooking. Find out which diseases and illnesses these herbs have traditionally been used to help or cure.

2 Ask an adult to help you to make these medieval recipes.
a) Bake apples in the oven and flavour them with honey and cinnamon.
b) Make **drawn gruel** by chopping and boiling lean beef with oatmeal, parsley, sage and salt. Add beaten egg yolks to thicken.
c) To make **pain perdu**, dip small slices of white bread into beaten egg yolks, fry them in butter and then spread them thickly with sugar or honey.

3 You could invite your friends to a Domesday party and give them medieval food to eat. Perhaps they could dress up in medieval clothes as well – you will find plenty of ideas for these in the pictures in this book.

4 Try to visit a farm where rare and old breeds of animals are reared and kept.

Looking after Domesday Book

Until about 1180, Domesday Book's home was the royal treasury at Winchester. Then London became the capital city of England, and Domesday was taken, with other valuable documents, treasure and jewels, to the abbey and palace of Westminster. The book was also often taken to places like York and Lincoln to be used in official business.

By about 1600, Domesday Book was in the Tally Court, Westminster, and in the 1740s it was moved to the Chapter House, Westminster, where it stayed until 1859. Since then it has been at the Public Record Office, Chancery Lane, London, apart from a trip to Southampton to be photographed in the 1860s, evacuations to Bodmin and Shepton Mallet prisons in the First and Second World Wars, and a spell at the Public Record Office, Kew from 1984 to early 1986 for repair and rebinding.

The Chapter House at Westminster in 1859.

How it was looked after

For most of its nine centuries, Domesday Book has been kept very securely. In the seventeenth and eighteenth centuries, it was in a heavy wood and iron chest with three locks. Its recent museum cases have been specially designed with strength and safety in mind.

At least since the 1630s, and probably long before that, there have been strict rules about handling Domesday Book, and these rules still apply today. No one is allowed to put his or her fingers or hands on the writing in case it gets smudged. This rule is vital, as the book itself shows. The corners of the pages are smooth and supple where the oil from human hands over the years has seeped into the parchment, and the few pieces of writing in the bottom corners of some pages have been almost worn away.

The bindings

Since the first binding, which was done shortly after King William's death, Domesday has been rebound on six occasions. The first was in the fourteenth century, the second in the sixteenth, and around 1600 metal decorations were put on the covers of both volumes. The book was rebound twice in the nineteenth century (1819 and 1869) and twice again in the twentieth (1953 and 1985). It has now been divided into five parts instead of two volumes to reduce wear and tear on the manuscripts and to let them be displayed more easily.

Some narrow escapes

Despite the strict rules about Domesday Book's handling and safety for many centuries, it has had some near misses.

In 1216 King John lost his baggage train and crown jewels in the Wash. Luckily, Domesday Book had been left behind.

In 1751 the Chapter House roof collapsed and could have crushed Domesday Book.

In 1819 woodworm was discovered in Domesday Book's covers, but not the parchment.

In 1834 Domesday Book was nearly burned down with the Houses of Parliament. Fortunately, the wind changed direction just in time.

In 1939 Domesday Book was left in an unguarded lorry in the Market Place at Shepton Mallet for half an hour when it was on its way to the prison for safe-keeping. The driver thought he was too early to arrive at the prison, so he went off to a café for tea. Luckily no one knew what was in the lorry!

Woodworm!

Fire!

Teabreak!

Things to find out and do

1 Design a new cover for Domesday Book. Would you put a different design on each of the five parts or not? The pictures show some early book cover designs to give you some ideas.

2 Try to see a **facsimile** (copy) of Domesday Book, or, better still, go to visit the original at the Public Record Office, Chancery Lane. What do you think about the way it is displayed? Would you do it differently?

Domesday quiz

When you have read this book and done some of the projects and activities suggested, you will have gained a great deal of knowledge about life in Norman England and Domesday Book itself. Test yourself by answering the questions below – the answers can all be found somewhere in these pages.

1 About how many words are there in Domesday Book?
2 What language is Domesday Book written in?
3 How many volumes and parts does Domesday Book have?
4 Why was Great Domesday left uncompleted?
5 About how many people were there in Domesday England?
6 How much of England was wooded in 1086?
7 What was the quickest way to travel in Domesday England?
8 What nearly happened to Domesday Book in 1834?
9 How did Domesday Book get its name?
10 What was the Danelaw?
11 How did William win at Hastings?
12 What was a villein?
13 How would you make *pain perdu*?
14 What features could you expect to see in a Norman church?
15 Who was at the bottom of the feudal ladder?
16 Name three kinds of people who are not included in Domesday Book.
17 How many oxen were there in an average ploughteam?
18 What does 'waste' mean when it refers to land?
19 How many times has Domesday Book been rebound?
20 What will be the date of the 1000 year anniversary of Domesday?

Other Domesday books

Do you want to find out if your town or village is mentioned in Domesday book? You can ask for the following books at your local library or look in a bookshop for them.

Facsimiles and translations

A **facsimile** is a copy of the original pages of a book. Domesday Book facsimiles look like the extracts shown in this book (in 11th century handwriting and Latin), so you will also need a translation to be able to follow the facsimile. However, you might like to see what your local entries actually looked like in the original Domesday Book.

There are two main facsimile editions of Domesday Book. One was made by the Ordnance Survey department, Southampton, between 1861 and 1863 and the second was made by Alecto Historical Edictions from 1986.

The Alecto Historical Editions volumes also have translations in English. Almost all of these translations are available separately in the *Victoria History of the Counties of England*.

A useful simplified English translation of Domesday Book is published by Phillimore in county volumes. The Latin text (as edited by Abraham Farley in 1783) runs beside the English translation.

Further books

P. Boyden, *The Children's Book of Domesday England* (1985) tells you about Domesday Book and life in medieval England.

T. Hinde (editor), *The Domesday Book: England's heritage then and now* (1985) looks at places mentioned in Domesday Book county by county, with photographs of what they are like now.

A complete list of all the books about Domesday Book can be found in D. Bates, *Domesday Bibliography* (1986).

Acknowledgments

The author and publishers wish to thank the following: Mrs Susan Lumas at the Public Record Office; Eira Reeves for original illustrations; for other illustrations: Aerofilms Ltd (p 21); Crown Copyright, Public Record Office (p 28); Editions Alecto (Domesday) Ltd (pp 9, 12); Historic Buildings and Monuments Commission for England (English Heritage) (p 5 bottom); the Phaidon Press Ltd (pp 4, 5 middle, 24 middle, 26); W. C. Saunders Esq. (p 24 bottom); Ronald Sheridan's Photo-Library (pp 2, 20, 23, 24 top).

Answers to Domesday facts on page 14

1 False. Domesday Book does not give us a complete description of life in the eleventh century, although it is of great help if we want to make one ourselves.
2 False. Different classes of people are mentioned and their numbers are often given, but there are many gaps. It is the men who are usually listed, not the women and children, except in the case of slaves. Nor are knights and retainers in castles or nuns and monks in monasteries mentioned.
3 False. A few families can trace their ancestry back to Domesday, but there are no pedigrees in its pages.
4 False. Domesday Book is attractive to look at, but it was a government document – it did not need to be decorated.
5 True. Most counties fill one or more complete quires.
6 True. However, many of the words are abbreviated to save space. The impression is rather like that of a modern restaurant guide or estate agent's details.
7 True.
8 True. Domesday Book is now easier to display and handle as it is bound in smaller sections than before.

ISBN 0 340 39732 2

First published 1986

Typeset in Gill medium by Facet Creative Studios Ltd.

Printed in Great Britain for Hodder and Stoughton Educational, a division of Hodder and Stoughton Ltd, Mill Road, Dunton Green, Sevenoaks, Kent by Chigwell Press, Loughton, Essex.